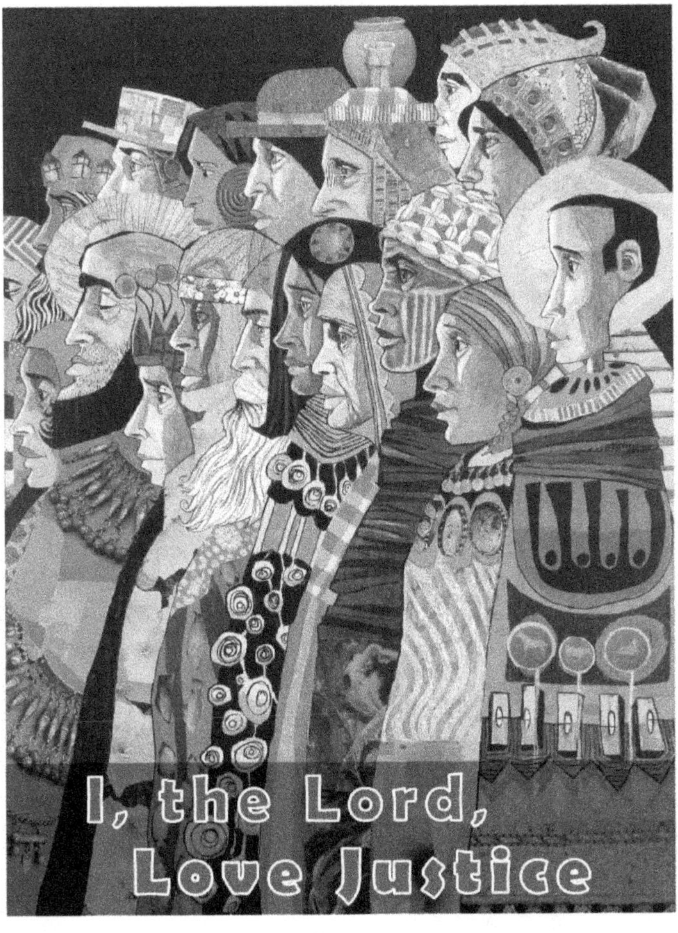

I, the Lord, Love Justice

Discussion Questions for 15 Bible Passages

Rev. Evan L. Keller

Beloved Communities Inc
DeLand, Florida

I, the Lord, Love Justice: Discussion Questions for 15 Bible Passages

Copyright © 2021 by Beloved Communities Inc.

All rights reserved. No parts of this book may be reproduced in any form without written permission from Beloved Communities Inc.

Published by:

Beloved Communities Inc
1702 N Woodland Blvd #116433
DeLand FL 32720
World Wide Web: www.beloved-communities.org
E-mail: info@beloved-communities.org
ISBN 978-1-7355656-5-1

Printed in the United States of America

Contents

Bible Study Guides
   Leviticus 25:1-38 --- 1
   Esther 4:1–17 -- 3
   Psalm 10:1-18 --- 5
   Isaiah 1:15–2:5 -- 7
   Isaiah 58:1-14 --- 9
   Isaiah 61:1-11 -- 15
   Isaiah 65:17–25 -- 17
   Jeremiah 22:1-17 -- 19
   Lamentations 3:1-66 --- 23
   Daniel 9:1-19 --- 27
   Amos 5:6-24 -- 29
   Luke 10:25-37 --- 31
   Acts 10 and Jonah 1 --- 33
   1 John 3:10-24; 4:7-21 -------------------------------------- 35
   Selected Scriptures --- 39

Appendix of Bible Study Tools
   Suggested Meeting Outline ---------------------------------- 45
   Preparing Your Bible Study -------------------------------- 47
   What is Inductive Bible Study? -------------------------- 49
   Asking Effective Questions -------------------------------- 57
   Bonding Questions --- 59
   Evaluating My Bible Study Facilitation ----------------- 63
   Facilitator vs. Commander --------------------------------- 69

Connecting with Beloved Communities Inc ---------------- 71
Works Cited --- 75

Bible Study Guides

Leviticus 25:1-38

1. Why does God command a seventh year of rest for the land?

2. What should we learn from God's care for the earth and our healthy relationship to it? (We are called to stewardship, not exploitation. Our relationship with the earth is important and is meant to be mutually beneficial.)

3. Why did God find it important for a family not to permanently lose its own property in the land of promise? How might that value in God's heart apply today?

4. Why does God connect protecting human land ownership with rest for the land? Imagine you are an Israelite whose family lost its land after your father suffered a lengthy illness and was not able to plant crops. What would the year of Jubilee mean to you?

5. There is no historical record of these jubilee laws ever being followed. What do you think made it harder to obey than other laws that became firmly embedded in Jewish culture?

6. Why is land ownership so crucial to economic freedom and wealth creation?

7. Why or why not were your parents and grandparents able to build equity in real estate?

8. How well has our country reflected God's value that each family acquire and retain property? Verse 10 says to

"proclaim liberty throughout the land to all its inhabitants."

9. How do these jubilee commands constitute liberty for all?

10. Read verse 23-24. How do you reconcile this passage's emphasis on land ownership with God's ultimate ownership stated here?

11. What must the Israelites not do to the poor? (Verses 14, 17, 36, 37). What are some ways these commands could be kept today? How is the promise of verses 21-22 counterintuitive? What does it teach us about God's work and our work?

12. Why do urban homes not revert to the original owners in the year of jubilee?

13. Read verse 38. What is the significance of this verse and why is it placed at the end of this chapter?

Esther 4:1-17

1. Give the group background of who Mordecai is. (Mordecai was a Jewish exile who worked as a court official for the Persian king Ahasuerus. After his cousin Esther's parents died, he adopted her. See Esther 2:5-7, 19-23.)

2. List all of the things Mordecai did in this passage.

3. What kind of person does what Mordecai did in this chapter? (take initiative, is bold and courageous, does homework, builds alliances, seeks justice from those in power, protects the vulnerable, is a leader.)

4. Before we get to Mordecai's famous challenge to Esther in verses 13-14, what do you make of their conversation through messengers in verses 4-12?

5. Will someone please put verse 14 in her or his own words?

6. Verse 14 is rich with timeless truths. What have these words of Mordecai revealed to God's people in every generation since then? (Like Esther's beauty and position as queen, each person's gifts are to be used to serve the common good - especially those who are vulnerable.)

7. How did Esther respond and what did it reveal about her character? (She responded by both fasting and organizing action.)

8. In verses 1-3 and 16, Mordecai and Esther fasted publicly and involved many others with them. What can we learn from that and how should we apply it in our own efforts for justice for the poor? (We think of fasting as a private personal practice of spiritual devotion.)

Psalm 10:1-18

1. What is the attitude of the wicked toward God in verses 2-6? (They deceived themselves into believing that God will not judge oppression. Their pride and arrogance attempt to usurp the place of God.)

2. How does pride lead to oppression? (Without apparent accountability or faith in God to provide a moral compass, the wicked are unrestrained in their greedy oppression.)

3. Their immunity to accountability is a mere mirage. How and when does God judge the wicked? (Reap what they have sown: verse 2. Direct intervention: verse 14,15,18. Final judgment: elsewhere in Scripture.)

4. Reread verses 7-10. What weapons do the wicked use against the poor? (deception and secrecy)

5. How do the wicked use deception and secrecy to oppress the poor? What are some current and historical examples? What big lies in our history have been the most damaging to people of color? (White supremacy which has been used as justification for slavery, segregation, mass incarceration, etc.)

6. Read John 3:19-20. How can we expose evil to the light?

7. Verses 1 and 12 are fervent prayers for God to intervene. How does God answer the cry for justice? (He *sees* their "trouble and grief": verse 14. He *hears* their cry: verse 17.

He encourages their hearts: verse 17. He intervenes to stop the oppressor: verse, 14,15,18.)

8. Although God the Father doesn't have physical eyes and ears, Jesus perfectly embodies God's heart for the humble. How do we see Jesus physically interacting with the suffering?

9. We are part of God's answer to Psalm 10's prayer for justice. Being followers of this compassionate Christ, what steps can we take to better see, hear, and empathize with the vulnerable?

10. What types of prayer from this passage can help the oppressed to put their trust in God? (As a prayer of lament, Psalm 10 models honest questions about why God hasn't intervened – verse 1, complaints about the oppressors – verse 2-11, requests for God to act on behalf of the oppressed – verse 12, requests for God to break the power of oppressors – verse 2,15, affirmations of God's heart for the poor – verse 14,16-18, and expressions of trust in God – verse 14.)

Isaiah 1:15–2:5

1. Look at verses 16-17. What are some of the nine verbs in God's rapid-fire commands?

2. Why do you think he compresses so many demands in rapid succession?

3. If verses 15-17 was the only divine instruction of how to live, what would a godly life look like?

   a. Turning from exploitive practices.

   b. Stopping others from oppressing the vulnerable.

   c. Emphasizing public justice rather than only private prayers.

   d. Healthy fellowship with God requires healthy fellowship with the poor.

4. Gods' call to repent continues in verses 18-31. Why does God appeal to reason in verses 18? (Turning from sinful injustice will be good for former oppressors as well as for the oppressed: choose blessing or judgment. Be smart!)

5. Greed is often the primary motive to exploit others. While economic exploitation has its benefits, how does it actually hurt its perpetrators as well as its victims? Do you have a current or historical example? Does the passage hint at any answers to this question?

a. When God is against you, you won't enjoy your ill-gotten gain (verse 31).

b. You may find your way to an early grave (verses 20, 24, 28, 31).

c. God may cause you to lose what you have taken from others (verses 22, 25).

d. Corruption makes life more risky, costly, and complicated for everyone (verse 23).

e. Your soul and conscience will be damaged by your injustice (verse 29).

6. There is a sudden switch in tone. Would a volunteer please read 2:1-5 for us? How did the flip switch from chapter one to chapter two? What changed and why is God so optimistic and determined to bring beauty out of our sin?

7. Which of these promises would you like us to be previews of in our community and how?

Isaiah 58:1-14

Note: Such a rich passage requires a longer study to explore fully. If you have more than 45 minutes, you could add in some of the "optional" questions. Another option is to split it into two studies.

1. If you had to divide this passage into two sections, where would you draw the line and what would you title each half? (verses 1-7 and verses 8-14)

2. Please scan the first half of the passage and call out some of the actions Isaiah instructs his hearers to take. (Two quartets of verbs are central to what God expects of his people in this passage: verse 6 tells us to: loose, untie, set free, and break. Verse 7 tells us to: share, provide, clothe, not turn away from. Verse 6 verbs tell us to stop practicing injustice. Verse 7 tells us to start showing mercy.)

3. What is wrong with their fasting? Why is God so upset? (Instead of truly seeking God in humility, which is the essence of fasting, they were making a show of being religious which didn't soften their hearts towards others. True humility lowers self below others rather than oppressing them. They were "expressing spiritual devotion without practical compassion" – Rev. Larry Kirk of Christ Community Church of Daytona Beach, Florida)

4. Optional question: Let's list the sins of commission, then the sins of omission that God is decrying. (<u>Commission</u>: exploit all your workers – verse 3, quarreling and strife –

verse 4, and striking with wicked fists – verse 4. <u>Omission</u>: rebel – verse 1, doesn't do right – verse 2, forsakes commands – verse 2, and does as you please – verse 3.) Which of these sins have you or are you struggling with?

5. What version of Israel's disconnect do we experience in our churches and lives? In other words, how is our own worship often hypocritical?

6. According to verses 6-10, what does true fasting - or true worship - entail in God's eyes? (See verses 6-7 and 9-10.)

7. How is breaking a yoke different from merely untying it temporarily? What would it mean to "do away with the yoke of oppression"? (Note Isaiah's phrases "chains of injustice" and "cords of the yoke". Yokes were heavy wooden stocks that helped force oxen to plow fields. Yokes are useful for oxen, but not appropriate for humans. Such unrelenting restriction of freedom is below our dignity as creatures made in God's image. We're not meant to be slaves, but to express our full humanity and creativity as stewards of God's world. "Chains of injustice" – verse 6, or "yokes of oppression" – verse 9, are societal sins that restrict the hope and human dignity of entire societies, such as gang extortion in Honduras, racial discrimination in the United States, or a fatalistic mindset in Haiti. In this chapter, God is saying that rooting out personal sins isn't enough. He wants us to root out societal sins that oppress the poor and vulnerable. The IVP Bible Background Commentary says "The picture is one of complete destruction of the means of oppression." - page 420.)

8. How would it look for our group to obey the command in verse 9 to "spend yourselves in behalf of the hungry and satisfy the needs of the oppressed"?

Isaiah 58:1-14

9. Read verses 3 and 9. Notice the difference in God's posture towards Israel from verse 3 to verse 9. Why do acts of justice for the poor bring God near? (When we act on God's heart, we draw near to him and become more like him.) How have you experienced this in your own life?

10. When people obey God's call in this chapter to add public justice to their personal piety, He makes some astounding promises to them in verses 8-14. They are beautifully and poetically expressed – like Amanda Gorman's poetry! What are some key promises to those who break the yoke of oppression? Call out phrases that you want to be true for you!

11. Now that we've experienced the powerful poetry of these promises, let's try to list out the main benefits God promises to bestow. How would you summarize these promises in a sentence or two? (I will draw near and fulfill your needs for joy and provision – verses 8,11,14; you will reflect me in a way that keeps blessing others as the following images reveal: light, righteousness, glory, garden, spring, rebuilder, repairer, restorer – verses 8,11,12. These promises aren't merely *presents from* God, but rather signs of the *presence of* God permeating all of life!)

12. Optional question: What is the gap between your life and the life described herein?

13. Optional question: The prophecy of Isaiah was written to a community, not an individual. Because of the individualistic lens of our culture, we often miss the implications of Scripture for a community of faith. How do you hope our own group will embody these blessings as we engage in God-pleasing justice for the poor? (Hints at community are found in verse 10's "yourselves" and verse 12's "your people.")

14. Optional question: How will we reflect God to the world as we live this blessed life together?

15. Calling folks to repent of oppression is not a popular message. That's why we need verse 1 to tell us to get loud, to "open your mouth and say something". It will be resisted, making it all the more urgent. Verse 14 says we'll be doing lots of rebuilding ruins, repairing walls, and restoring streets. The struggle for racial justice in the United States has often required rebuilding prior gains that have been torn down by backlashes of White supremacy. This has been true after Reconstruction, the Civil Rights Movement, and the administration of our first African American President. Triumph is often followed by tragedy. This can erode our hope and stir up anger. How can we gain strength for the struggle from the promises of this passage?

16. Optional question: How does this passage speak into the idea of burnout in the intense work for justice? (God renews us as we act on His heart for the lost and vulnerable. In John 4:34, Jesus said "My food is to do the will of my Father and to finish his work.")

17. Optional question: How does the practice of Sabbath in verse 13 tie in with the theme of the passage as a whole?

18. Optional question: Since the Old Testament points ahead to Jesus, how does He embody this passage?

19. How would you summarize the message of this passage? (True worship is acting on God's heart, leveraging all you are and have to serve others, especially the vulnerable. Pastor Mark Labberton writes that "Justice and mercy are not add-ons to worship, nor are they the consequences of worship. Justice and mercy are intrinsic to God and therefore intrinsic to the worship of God....*We should not fool*

Isaiah 58:1-14

ourselves into thinking that it's enough to feel drawn to the heart of God without our lives showing the heart of God." – The Dangerous Act of Worship, page 38.)

20. Who are the poor we have turned away from? What actions for justice could we undertake together? (Have a volunteer take notes or write a list on a whiteboard, then pray through your list.)

21. Corporate prayer. Let's seek God's blessing as we seek to obey His Word by practicing justice and mercy. As we pray, let's remember to both repent of the sins of v.1-7 as well as claim the promises of verses 8-14. So, you might want to pray with your Bibles open.

Notes on the cultural context of a few phrases we no longer use today:

- Verse 8's "go before you" and "be your rear guard" would remind the Israelites of the pillar of cloud and fire that accompanied them in the wilderness as a sign of God's presence and direction.

- Verse 12's references to rebuilding ruins may be related to Isaiah's prophecy that Jerusalem would be destroyed and that God's people would be forced into exile in Babylon for a time. "Many ancient cities were rebuilt after having been destroyed...often more splendid than before" (IVP Bible Background Commentary, page 638).

- Verse 14's to "ride on the heights of the land" "speaks of victory and security" (IVP Bible Background Commentary, page 638) and of "triumphant conquerors" (Edward Young's commentary The Book of Isaiah, page 427.)

Isaiah 61:1-11

1. When Jesus was handed the scroll of Isaiah in the synagogue at Capernaum, He chose the first two verses of chapter 61 to read, then declared: "Today this scripture is fulfilled in your hearing" (Luke 4:21). As He was launching His ministry, He may have been claiming this as His mission statement. What ideas in this chapter do you see fulfilled in Jesus?

2. In verses 3-9 who do "they" or "their" refer to? (mostly to verse 3's "those who mourn in Zion")

3. What references does this passage make to Israel's exile in Babylon? (captives in verse 1, Zion's mourning in verse 3, rebuilding ruins in verse 4, shame in verse 7, and land in verse 7) The passage is mostly forward looking; what promises does the Anointed One make to the exiles?

4. Scholars call this a Messianic song because of its joy and its poetic structure. Call out verse numbers and phrases that relate to joy or flourishing. In a world of such brokenness and evil, why is this passage so optimistic? (The Messiah is announcing an abundance of good news that will in time restore everything.)

5. It's rare for the Bible to state that God loves something other than people. According to verse 8, what does God love and hate? How does He act on this and how does this shape your view of God?

6. Remember that biblical righteousness is closely related to justice and refers to public holiness: serving the common good in a way that pleases God. What metaphors for righteousness are used in this chapter and what do they say about it? (trees in verse 3, robe in verse 10, and sprouting seed in verse 11). Which image (tree, robe, sprout) do you want to better embody in your own public righteousness?

7. Skim back over the passage to see which actions are done by people and what God Himself does. Let's make two lists (on a whiteboard, if available). What is the relationship between human and divine action on behalf of the vulnerable? (Hint: explore verses 1 and 8.) How will your efforts for biblical justice be influenced by the truth that God's people are agents of God's good future?

8. What aspects of the Messianic mission of verses 1-9 would you like to participate more in?

9. In verses 10-12, the voice shifts from the Anointed One to the response of God's people to His good news. What images are used and what do they communicate?

10. Take time to praise God for promises of this Messianic song that are already being fulfilled, and to pray for the restoration still to come.

Isaiah 65:17–25

What is the mood of this passage and how does it make you feel? (Joy, creation, newness, flourishing, peace, fairness, and longevity.)

1. God promises that 11 currently common occurrences will not be part of his new creation. What are some of these?
2. Read verses 21-22. Please expound on these promises. Why are they so important to human flourishing and how are they different from what the poor experience today?
3. How would today's poor or Israelite exiles in Isaiah's day react to the picture this passage paints?
4. What do the animal metaphors in verse 25 mean for people?
5. Joy is a running theme in this passage. Who is happy and why? (God and thriving people both rejoice in the good human habitat that God creates.)
6. How would you summarize the good life you see in this passage? (Longevity, fruitful labor, and physical security.)
7. List all of the harmonious relationships you can find in this passage. (God and His people, people and the rest of creation, between people, between animals.)
8. Has God already started this new creation and what evidence supports your answer?

9. What role can we play in God's new creation, if any? What do this and other passages say on this question? ("We are God's fellow workers" - 1 Corinthians 3:9.)

10. How will prayer be transformed in the new creation?

11. What can we do as a community to reflect this coming reality today?

Jeremiah 22:1-17

1. Who is this passage addressed to specifically ("the king of Judah" – verse 1) and why? (Power brings additional opportunity for both justice and injustice.)

2. We often have more power than we realize. How can you use yours to do justice and fight injustice?

3. God's covenant with the ancient Jewish people repeatedly required special concern for strangers, orphans, and widows, including gleaning laws that provided food for the poor, kinsman redeemer laws that cared for widows, and Jubilee laws that provided economic justice. And since God's Word is for every nation in every generation, let's think about how it applies to us. Who are the people of verse 3? In today's world...

    a. Who has been "robbed by the hand of the oppressor"? (Underpaid laborers)

    b. Who is "the stranger"? (Immigrants, refugees, people on lowest rungs of a racial hierarchy)

    c. Who is "the orphan"? (Orphans, children of the incarcerated, victims of police brutality)

    d. Who is "the widow"? (Vulnerable, unheard, unemployed, underemployed, uninsured)

4. Let's list all the verbs in verse 3. What are the actions we are told to do or not do? (Do justice and righteousness, deliver, do not mistreat or do violence, do not shed innocent blood.) What do these actions entail and how could we do them here locally? (Doing "what is right and just" is repeated in verses 3, 13, and 15. In fact, you'll find that "righteousness and justice" is a common pair in the Old Testament. See the "Explanation of Biblical Righteousness and Justice" at the end of the Amos 5 study.)

5. This passage promises blessings to Israel and its kings for doing justice for the vulnerable, but also promises destruction and exile to the unjust. We know that oppressors gain economically from exploiting others, but we don't always see the bad fruit they reap from their wicked seeds. From both this passage and your own real-life observations, what do oppressors gain and what do they lose through their oppression? (Help them explore the passage's promised blessings in verses 4, 15-16 and promised punishments in verses 5-13. If the group doesn't mention it, point out how doing good increases relational harmony with God and others, and builds Christlike character – all of which produce joy. And, of course, oppression produces the opposite of each of those gains.)

6. What lessons does Isaiah intend to teach through the image of a King building a palace. (Much like our use of "the White House", the "king's house" was a metaphor for the entire administration of the kingdom – extending the metaphor that justice be the foundation of both the physical house and the governmental house. Because the king did not pay his construction laborers, his wealthy regime was tainted through forced labor.)

7. Why does God hate low or no wages?

Jeremiah 22:1-17

8. In verse 17, Isaiah comes right out and names the sin of greed which we see at work in his image of a king building a palace through forced labor. What decisions are you tempted to make that would harm others for financial gain? (Examples may include: sweatshop products, retailers or contractors who pay less than a living wage, investments that support unethical companies, not giving a good tip to a low-wage worker who serves you.)

9. Read verse 14-15. What misconceptions about material things does this verse correct? (A person's value is not determined by their "net worth," nor is possessing wealth evil in itself.) Please raise your hand if you've ever considered someone less valuable because of their economic or social status? How can that sin be rooted out of our mindsets?

10. Read verse 16. How is doing justice for the poor equivalent to knowing God? (Caring for the poor reflects God's heart and thus creates intimacy with Him as our hearts beat with His concerns.)

11. Let's pray now for God to so shape our actions that our hearts are drawn into intimacy with His heart for His broken world. Let's ask for His strength to act on applications of this passage we have discussed related to greed, economic justice, doing what is right and just for the vulnerable, and valuing people aside from their material wealth.

Lamentations 3:1-66

1. Who is "he" who afflicted the poet in verses 1-17?

2. Read verses 31-33. In what sense is God the cause of His people's suffering?

3. Read verses 44-45. Why has God allowed some ethnic groups to suffer centuries of oppression?

4. What things does the poet remember in verses 19-21? (How his long and bitter affliction is softened the Lord's faithful love)

5. Why is it so important for everyone to remember the bitter truths in their history?

6. In Hebrew poetry, placing a theme in the middle of a poem is a key way to highlight its importance.

7. So, in the middle of this passage (verses 22-23) we find the most well-known saying in Lamentations. This reminder of God's faithfulness in the midst of suffering follows the pattern of biblical prayers of lament which honestly cry out to God in pain, but also reaffirm trust in God. How does remembering God's love affect the poet? (It gives him hope in despair as he remembers the unchanging attributes of God, particularly His love, compassion, and faithfulness.)

8. How does the poet hold fast to this belief while suffering such afflictions?

9. What fresh expressions of God's faithful love have you experienced?

10. Read verses 24-26. What does it mean to wait for God? And how can you do so when the waiting lasts for generations?

11. What reasons for hope does the poet see in verses 31-38?

    a. (Reasons for hope cited by the Africa Bible Commentary on p.929:

    b. God takes no pleasure in suffering – verse 33;

    c. His judgments are carried out with compassion verses 31-32;

    d. He sees all the evil that is done under the sun, including what Babylon has done to Israel – verses 34-36;

    e. He will bring justice because He is the true Ruler of all – verses 37-38.)

12. Read verse 40-42. How does self-examination and confession fit into this poem of affliction?

13. Verses 45-66 complain about enemies and ask God to judge them. How does this relate to the biblical command to forgive those who sin against us?

14. The book of Lamentations is often attributed to Jeremiah. Verses 52-63 has parallels to Jeremiah's experience of being thrown in a pit then rescued by an Ethiopian servant of the King (Jeremiah 38: 1-13). What can we learn from how the Lord met him during this trial?

15. How does the African American experience echo this poem of lament?

16. What roles can this poem play in the lives of American people of color?
17. What roles can this poem play in the lives of White Americans?
18. How does Jesus fulfill this poem of lament? (The New Bible Commentary, p.713: "There is great poignancy in the fact that the suffering poet bore the griefs of the people, even as he suffered at their hands. There are obvious similarities with the song about the Suffering Servant in Isaiah 52-53 and there is a foreshadowing of the insults and cruelty heaped on Jesus Christ by the people He came to save, even as He showed in Himself the deep compassions of God for them.")

Carson, D.A. (1953). *New Bible Commentary*. Leicester: Inter-Varsity Press.
Adeyemo, T. (2006). *Africa Bible Commentary*. Nairobi: Zondervan.

Daniel 9:1-19

1. What can we learn from Daniel's relationship with God? (He reads his Bible, claims God's promises, and asks God to fulfill His Word – using Scripture in his prayer.)

2. To what extent has Daniel been immersed in and shaped by the Hebrew Scriptures? How would you like to better follow his example?

3. What is the historical context that shapes Daniel's response? (God's covenant people Israel, of which he is a part, have rebelled by practicing hundreds of years of idolatry and injustice. God sent many prophets (verse 6) including Jeremiah whose prophecy Daniel is reading, to warn of his coming judgment if they do not repent. The destruction of Jerusalem by enemy nations, namely Babylon and Assyria, and the exile and subjugation of the Israelites by those nations is the ultimate punishment by which God brings Israel to a place of humble repentance. Daniel is one of these exiles in Babylon, and his prayer here is part of the repentance that God is seeking.)

4. Whose sins does he confess? Why does he feel a sense of responsibility for sins his ancestors committed scores and hundreds of years ago?

5. Given that God ties us to Adam and Eve's original sins, how is the Bible's view of corporate identity, shame and guilt different from our modern, American individualism?

6. How should we follow Daniel's example of owning up to the sins of our own nation?

7. Read verse 3. How intensely does Daniel pray for his people? Why do we not pray with such fervency for our own nation?

8. Scan verses 15-19 and tell us some of the words you see repeated over and over. Notice that the word "your" is repeated 18 times in these five verses. What are some nouns he puts after "your"? (People, anger, fury, city, mountain, servant, face, sanctuary, ear, eyes, name, and mercies.)

9. What is Daniel getting at by making his prayer about God?

10. What kind of prayers and actions should our group undertake to be true to this passage? As Daniel did, let's use Scripture in our prayers. Feel free to repeat and expand upon any of these verses as the Holy Spirit leads you.

Amos 5:6-24

1. What images does Amos use in verses 6-9 and what mood do they communicate? (This is serious – the all-powerful God will judge you if you disobey, so conduct yourselves accordingly.)

2. What does "in the gate" mean in verses 10, 12, and 15? (In the gate refers to the seat of power. Judges who represent the king would literally sit in the city gate and settle disputes between citizens.)

3. What is God so upset about in verse 7 and 10-12? (see note below on biblical righteousness and justice). What would these sins look like today – locally, nationally, and internationally?

4. Let's look at what God wants. Read verses 14-15: What would it look like for us as God's people to "seek good and not evil" and to "hate evil, love good"? According to verses 14-15 who benefits when we do good to others?

5. Although this passage is heavier on judgment than blessing, what promises does he give to the obedient? (That you may live – verses 6, 14, opposite of verse 11's judgments are applied. Also, Lord "will be with you" verse 14 and be gracious – verse15.)

6. What is wrong with Israel's religious practices in verses 21-23?

7. Is the judgment threatened in this passage inflicted only when the future day of the Lord comes (verses 18, 20) or is it meted out to oppressors here and now?

8. How would oppressors be better off if they practice righteousness and justice instead?

9. What makes verse 24 such a powerful command? Why has it been such a rallying cry in movements for justice? What does it mean? (Ongoing systemic abundance that benefits all.) What light does the context of this entire chapter shed upon this famous verse?

10. How would our city be different if verse 24 were true here?

11. How can we pray and work toward that end?

Explanation of Biblical Righteousness and Justice:

"The words justice and righteousness constitute a 'hendiadys,' one idea in two words. When Amos pairs justice – *mishpat* – with righteousness – *tsedek*, the prophet means a just, righteous rule, ordered by God's intention for the world, by God's economy. In God's just and righteous reign on earth, there is healing, harmony, wholeness; there is truly freedom, liberty, and justice for all." – Jacqui Lewis, senior minister at Middle Collegiate Church in New York, as quoted on page 24 of the January 2021 edition of Sojourners Magazine.

Luke 10:25-37

1. Verse 27 speaks of loving God with heart, soul, strength, and mind. How did the good Samaritan love God in these ways?

2. Read verse 28 and 37. If we are to love with heart, soul, strength, and mind, why does Jesus put so much emphasis on our actions?

3. What was the lawyer's first question? (verse 25.) The answer Jesus gave, "Do this and you will live" echoes the question and suggests a flourishing life even now. How would it fill us with life to give ourselves to those we are conditioned to avoid?

4. What is the lawyer's second question? (verse 29.) Jesus' answer is anything but straightforward, suggesting he was asking the wrong question. What question did Jesus answer instead? (How can I be a neighbor to those I've been taught to hate?)

5. A danger with familiar passages is to rest on our memory rather than taking a fresh look at the actual passage. So, let's take a minute to read verses 30-36 silently and look for one thing that stands out to you this time. (After a minute of silence, invite the group to share their insights.)

6. What is a Samaritan and what effect would making a hero out of one have had on the original hearers of Jesus' story?

7. What justifications for inaction did the priest and Levite likely make?

8. What similar justifications do we make for our own apathy towards those in need?

9. What are all the ways the Samaritan was a neighbor to the half dead man?

10. What role did the inn keeper play in restoring the victim's health and is there a present day parallel?

11. To whom is God calling us to show mercy?

Acts 10 and Jonah 1

1. Read Acts 10:1-8 and Jonah 1:1-3. What similarities do you see in these two stories? (God's messenger sails from Joppa with a message of repentance for people of the current oppressive world empire.)

2. Read Acts 10:44-48 and Jonah 3:1-4:11. How do the hated oppressors respond to the message about God and how does the messenger react? (Both repent. One messenger pouts alone and the other enjoys fellowship with glad and grateful new believers.)

3. If Jonah had chosen to rejoice in Nineveh's repentance, how do you picture his story ending differently?

4. How deeply rooted were Peter's beliefs about ethnic separation and what did it take to change his mindset? (A vision from God, a Gentile's encounter with God that pinpointed Peter's exact location, a God-fearing Gentile whose entire community was sincerely seeking God, and clear evidence that God filled these Gentiles with the Holy Spirit.)

5. What do the experiences of Jonah and Peter teach us about the difficult possibility of overcoming racial divisions?

6. Nineveh was the capital of a notoriously oppressive empire known for cruelly torturing its enemies, yet God calls it a

"great city" in the first and last sentences of the book of Jonah and once in between. Jonah saw it as irredeemable and eagerly awaited its destruction.

7. Although our country has its own history of violent oppression, do we share God's vision for its transformation?

1 John 3:10-24; 4:7-21

Note: Depending on your timeframe, you can combine or separate these two studies.

1 John 3:10-24

1. What does it mean to "practice righteousness" as it says in verse 10?

2. What does John mean by "from the beginning" in verse 11?

    a. What pairs of contrasting ideas does John use in verse 10-18? (Children of God versus children of the devil. Love his brother versus slew his brother. Righteous deeds versus evil deeds. Life versus death. Love versus murder. Love in deed and truth versus love in word or with tongue.)

3. Read verse 11-13. Why does the world hate those who love and do what is right?

4. Read verse 16. Although we cannot die for each other's sins, how else can we lay down our lives for each other?

5. Read verses 17-18. How is sharing with a needy brother or sister a prime example of practicing righteousness, loving, and laying down our lives for our brothers and sisters?

6. What is John's point about the heart in verses 19-22?

7. Verse 23 joins belief in Jesus to loving one another. Why can't we have one without the other? (Verse 17 offers a clue in the phrase, "how does the love of God abide in him." It is God's love in us that enable us to truly love others, so as we draw near to God, His love flows through us stronger and purer. 1 John 4:7 say bluntly, "love is from God.")

8. The idea of abiding is a running theme in this passage – see verses 14, 15, and 24. He connects our "abiding" to death, eternal life, and Jesus. What does he mean by this and how does it relate to loving each other?

1 John 4:7-21

1. What are all the ways our love relies on the love of God revealed in the cross of Christ?

   - God's love regenerates us – by that love we are, "born of God" (4:7) and we "live through him" (verse 9).

   - The cross defines love for us, showing us that love is free and sacrificial to the point of death.

   - Receiving the ultimate gift of redeeming love, we are inspired to pass on such love out of gratitude for our own salvation (verse11).

   - Being united to Christ, we are infused with his love by his Spirit (verse 13). His love is "manifested in us" (verse 9).

2. What does it mean in verses 12 and 17-19 that "his love is perfected in us"?

3. How does that perfect love drive out fear? How should we apply this to our multiracial friendships?

4. What does it mean in verse 17 that "as he is, so also are we in this world"?

5. Would someone break down the logic of verse 24 for us?

6. Verse 21 ends our passage with a reminder that love for each other should flow from love for God. How does the idea of abiding – which is woven throughout this passage – provide the lifeblood for our love?

Selected Scriptures
(the questions)

Disclaimer: Most of our Bible studies look at verses in the immediate context of the passage they are found in, but today we study a group of verses from different books cautiously since doing so can raise the chances of misinterpretation. Encourage your group members to read the entire chapters on their own to get the fuller context. Proceed with caution!

1. What are some words and ideas that tie these passages together? (All/every, unity/one, in, Father and Son, and to a lesser degree: love, glory, and blood.)

2. What forms of speech do you see here? Which passages are prayers or statements or something else?

3. Why is unity expressed sometimes as a statement of fact and sometimes as a prayer? (There is a gap between our identity as one and our lived experience. God requires us to live into the truth of our oneness – hence the command of 1 Peter 3:8.)

4. What are some of the characteristics of our unity that you can see in these passages?

5. Why are the Father and Son paired together so often – especially in John 17? How is their relationship important to unity between believers?

6. The biblical writers seem to be using the word "in" in a special way. What do you think they're getting at and how does it relate to our oneness with each other? (The Father and Son are "in" each other in a mysterious way – a deep sharing of being that we are invited into. When Jesus bonds us to His Father, it creates the basis for our unity with each other. In other words, we are one with each other only as we become one with God. It is the deepest and most powerful bond between humans. It is unbreakable. We are family!)

7. Which of these versus hint at our family ties? Now we know that family isn't always pleasant! According to these verses, what is the family of God supposed to look like?

8. What event in redemptive history forged that unbreakable bond? Which of these verses highlight the cross and how do they tie the cross to unity? (Ephesians 2:13-15, Revelation 5:9.) How do these verses use the words glory and glorify? What brings God glory in these verses? Is glory a present or future reality?

9. Today's verses are the official Foundational Scriptures upon which Beloved Communities Inc is built. Let's take a look at these versus side-by-by side with our Beloved Communities' vision, mission and values (see below). Please point out the specific connections you see between our Foundational Scriptures and our vision, mission and values.

10. List some of the key actions in these passages. ["Dwell together in unity", "welcome one another", "live in harmony", "glorify God with one voice", 1 Peter 3:8.]

11. What specific actions can our beloved community take to better live out this biblical unity?

Selected Scriptures
(the passages)

Psalm 133:1 "Behold, how good and how pleasant it is for brothers [and sisters] to dwell together in unity!"

Matthew 6:10 "Your kingdom come, your will be done, on earth as it is in heaven."

John 17:20-23 "My prayer is not for them alone. I pray also for those who will believe in me through their message, that all of them may be one, Father, just as you are in me and I am in you. May they also be in us so that the world may believe that you have sent me. I have given them the glory that you gave me, that they may be one as we are one – I in them and you in me – so they may be brought to complete unity. Then the world will know that you sent me and have loved them even as you have loved me…"

Romans 12:5 "in Christ we who are many are one body, and each member belongs to one another."

Romans 15:5-7 "May the God of endurance and encouragement grant you to live in such harmony with one another, in accord with Christ Jesus, that together you may with one voice glorify the God and Father of our Lord Jesus Christ. Therefore welcome one another as Christ has welcomed you, for the glory of God."

Galatians 3:26-28 "So in Christ Jesus you are all children of God through faith, for all of you who were baptized into Christ have clothed yourselves with Christ. There is neither Jew nor Gentile, neither slave nor free, nor is there male and female, for you are all one in Christ Jesus."

Ephesians 2:13-14   "But now in Christ Jesus you who once were far away have been brought near through the blood of Christ. For He Himself is our peace, who has made the two one and has torn down the dividing wall of hostility."

1 Peter 3:8   "Finally, all of you, have unity of mind, sympathy, brotherly love, a tender heart, and a humble mind."

Revelation 5:9   "At the cost of blood you ransomed for God persons from every tribe, language, people and nation."

Appendix of Bible Study Tools

All appendix tools are available in digital format
as free downloads at:
www.Beloved-Communities.org

Suggested Meeting Outline

BEFORE
1. Use "Preparing My Bible Study" (in Appendix) to get yourself ready to lead an effective discussion.
2. Request all the logistical and in-meeting help you'll need from others (see checklist in "Preparing My Bible Study)." Share leadership as much as possible to create group ownership.
3. Ask a group member to fill-out the evaluation form in the Appendix: "Evaluating My Bible Study Facilitation."

DURING
1. Informal fellowship and refreshments.
2. Opening prayer.
3. Sharing time (possibly using a question from the Appendix: "Bonding Questions")
4. Read passage aloud.
5. Silent individual study – give them something to look for to observe the passage well.
6. Discuss bible study questions - identify ones that seem highest priority if time is short.
   a. See your role as steadily directing the group back to the passage to learn from it rather than only sharing their personal opinions.
   b. Be sensitive to how the Spirit is speaking to your group through the passage and discussion

– even if it leads the discussion in a direction you had not anticipated.
   c. See more discussion facilitation tips in the Appendix: "Evaluating My Bible Study Facilitation".
7. Summarize key themes from the passage/discussion. (Your co-facilitator could do this.)
8. Help identify specific individual and group applications.
9. Pray as a group in response to the passage and commit to appropriate actions in response. Encourage attendees to keep their Bibles open and refer to verses they've studied in their prayers.
10. Announce upcoming events (including four regular actions of a Beloved Community: bible study, justice book discussions, fellowship meals, and justice action).

AFTER
1. Fill out "Evaluating My Bible Study Facilitation" yourself and compare your perspective with what the other evaluator wrote.
2. Coordinate and/or remind the group of any applications they committed to.

Preparing Your Bible Study

1. Read the text, writing down the observations and questions that it sparks.

2. Research the context:
   a. textual context: author and themes/events in the rest of the book.
   b. cultural context: relevant geography – culture – history.

3. Try to answer the questions you wrote down, finding answers in the passage, the whole biblical book it is in, and Bible commentaries (after looking at Scripture itself first!).

4. Decide what you'll ask the group to look for in order to observe the passage well during the individual study time.

5. What is the main theme of the passage? Summarize it.

6. What are some Observation questions to focus the group on the passage?

7. What are some Interpretation questions that wrestle with the main truths of the passage?

8. What are some Application questions that can encourage real change?

9. If you're using a study guide, integrate its best questions with those you've just written.

10. Pray for your upcoming time together – with your co-facilitator if possible.

11. Use the "Suggested Meeting Outline" (in Appendix) as a starting point to plan the order and timeline of your gathering.

12. Choose a sharing question for your community-building time (Bonding Questions in the Appendix provide lots of possibilities).

13. Ask for help from others to lead segments of the meeting (praying, reading, sharing time, summarizing key themes from the passage/discussion) and logistics (food, drinks, location, meeting reminders, and giving feedback on your facilitating).

What is Inductive Bible Study?

Observe, Interpret, Apply.
These steps of inductive bible study are really just a natural sequence we follow in everyday situations. Skipping a step or going in the wrong order can be disastrous. Consider this scenario: If a ball bounces across the road in front of your vehicle, what do you observe, interpret, apply? Easy, right? If you're texting and don't see the ball, you'll fail to interpret that a child might be following it. You won't apply the brakes and you may end up facing criminal charges!

Natural or Not?
As natural as observe > interpret > apply is in some parts of our lives, when it comes to things we already have a fair amount of knowledge about, our brains often see what they want to see rather than what is actually there! Counterintuitively, this makes people who are unfamiliar with the Bible better at approaching Scripture inductively. Seasoned Christians may tend to rely on previous knowledge rather than taking a fresh look at the passage in front of them.

Taking Inductive to Court.
"Inductive" is the approach a jury is supposed to take. With an objective posture, they gather *all* evidence before drawing conclusions, whereas the attorneys in the case are decidedly "deductive," presuming innocence or guilt up front. They start with their conclusion, ignore or even hide some of the facts, and build a case around the remaining facts (and sometimes "alternative facts"). So, like a jury, inductive study stirs deep curiosity for God's Word.

We look closely and ask lots of questions of the text in order to know God better and align our lives with His will.

Your Main Job.
An inductive approach can level the playing field amongst varying levels of Bible knowledge while keeping the focus on learning from the Bible passage itself rather than from rehashed tidbits from years of fuzzily recalled sermons! But it takes steady work to steer the discussion in this direction, including a sprinkling of training over time, intentional leadership in each study, and gentle coaxing when the discussion sails off the rails. You may have noticed that many of the discussion questions in this booklet begin with "According to verses…" or "Read verses…" to steer groups back into the passage. In fact, that's a big part of your role: directing their attention to God's Word which has the unique power to deeply transform those who truly listen and obey. This puts the Bible rather than yourself at the center of the conversation. You keep bringing the discussion back to the passage, looking to the Bible itself rather than personal opinions for answers to the discussion questions. The goal of inductive study is to let the Bible speak for itself, reveal God to us, and help us align our lives with it.

Skipping Ahead.
Of the three steps of inductive study (observe, interpret, apply), which do you think is most often neglected? Our answer: observation. Why is that? In addition to the above reasons, we may find the supporting details too obvious, too hard to dig up, or too boring – we want to get practical right away. In fact, we tend to skip interpretation (what it means) as well, hopping directly to application (what it means *to me*). As the illustration of the ball bouncing across the road makes clear, not observing can quickly lead to misinterpreting and misapplying.

OBSERVE: Engaging Your Group.

What is Inductive Bible Study?

So, we suggest that in each study you gently nudge the group toward observation, such as by sharing one of the above illustrations (bouncing ball or jury vs. attorney). Another helpful approach is to give your group an observation assignment during the individual study time, such as: "As you read, please note the major turning points in the passage, or words that are repeated several times, or answer to the reporter questions: who/what/where/when/why/how." Those are three ideas – I suggest using only one of them per study. Often you can customize this to your passage – asking them to look for something important that you found in your own individual study time.

INTERPRET: One Big Key.
The second step, interpret, is usually the longest segment of the conversation. When it comes to interpreting well, context is king! What surrounds a word or sentence helps you see its fuller meaning, like knowing where someone lives helps your mind ground them in concrete reality. Take the simple statement: "Let's remove your appendix." It means one thing when your editor says it. If your surgeon says it, the meaning is quite a bit different! So who says what to whom plus when and where it is said have a big impact on its meaning.

Con-Text.
The immediate context of a scripture verse is what comes right before and right after. The broader context of a text includes the whole book of the Bible it is in, and all 66 books of the Bible. This bigger picture helps us understand what a verse is saying. As the saying goes: "Scripture interprets scripture." But be careful when referring to passages outside of the book your passage is in. Bible study leaders often sabotage the focus on their primary passage by diverting group attention to too many related passages. It's so tempting to point out every intriguing connection!

But ignoring the *immediate* context can distort your interpretation. For example, Paul's instruction for wives to be submissive in Ephesians 5:22 is informed by the immediately preceding command to "submit to one another" (v.21) and the revelation that a husband's love is to be sacrificial rather than domineering (v.25).

Another example is John 10:10. Who is the thief who "comes only to steal and kill and destroy"? Christians apply this phrase to Satan, of whom it is no doubt true. But a closer look at the context (John 10:8; 9:40-41) suggests that this verse is continuing Christ's ongoing critique of the Pharisees.

Get the Back Story.
So far, we've been talking only about textual context, yet another kind of context also breathes in meaning. Both the broader *text* and the broader *culture* help us understand a passage. Cultural context is the background on the people, places, and customs of the author's culture.

This suggests we should approach the bible with the same openness to learn as when visiting a new country for the first time. In fact, you actually *are* crossing cultures. The Bible's ancient Near East settings are quite different from your daily life, so it helps to try to enter a passage's cultural context rather than cramming it into your 21st century point of view.

Foot washing illustrates the need for cultural context. Knowing it was a necessary but lowly task usually done by servants infuses additional meaning into the act of Jesus washing his disciples' feet. This background turns this act into history's most vivid example of servant leadership.

What is Inductive Bible Study?

Crawling into the Original Ears.
Paying attention to the cultural background can give you a better sense of what your passage would have meant to its original hearers, which can guard against misinterpretations and deepen the contemporary meaning. For an example from a passage in this study guide, the original hearers would have heard "proclaim freedom for the captives" (Isaiah 61:1) as applying to the Hebrew captives in Babylon. With that knowledge, contemporary readers can see how serious a captivity the Messiah promises to deliver from. The exile to Babylon lasted 70 years, resulted in the confiscation of wealth, the destruction of cities, and the forced displacement of thousands of Jews. It threatened to obliterate the culture of an entire people. Hope for deliverance from such a powerful oppressor seemed dim. This background gives today's readers a vivid picture of the human injustice God hates as well as the power of the Messiah to break powerful spiritual captivity.

It's Like Time Travel.
With cultural context in mind, which do you think is harder…? For a first century person to understand Star Wars or a 21st century person to understand the Book of Revelation? Actually, quite a bit of cultural background is needed for both.
Here are some cultural cues a first century person would need to make sense of Star Wars:
- Film is a form of entertainment and it doesn't necessarily portray life realistically.
- The story is in a literary genre called science fiction, which is about the future, space, fantasy, and aliens.
- It's part of a series of several movies (greater context).
- These terms need defining: jedi, Nubian, lightsabre, pod racing and midichlorian.

Here are some cultural cues a 21st century person would need to make sense of Revelation:

- It's part of a genre of prophetic books that use highly symbolic language.
- The writer and recipients lived in a corrupt Roman Empire which hated Christians and often killed them.
- There are dozens of allusions to Old Testament symbols.
- It's a letter.
- The seven cities mentioned are in modern day Turkey.
- Seals on a scroll identify its author as well as guard the privacy of its contents.

Sum it Up.
Since the interpret step covers a lot of ground and can be messy, it is helpful to sum up for the group what the Lord has been speaking through His Word. Refer back to key insights from group members to reinforce that God is speaking through His people. Zooming back out to the big picture reminds members what they've learned about God. This is a good opportunity to look at how the passage points to Jesus, the center of Scripture and our faith.

Mixing Black & White Approaches.
Given the generally different Black and White approaches to group bible studies, we offer the following suggestion for how to summarize the discussion. We find that it helps everyone feel a bit more at home.

To over-generalize, White bible studies are heavy on analytical discussion and sharing of knowledge between all group members, while Black bible studies are more akin to sermons from the group leader as the respected authority. Both are legitimate approaches. The multiracial co-facilitators of our Beloved Communities should discuss their strengths and preferences with each other and ask the group which format they lean towards. Our "Beloved Communities" try to strike a balance between the two, infusing inductive bible study discussions with a strong summary which exhorts the Beloved

Community to faithfully integrate God's truth into their personal and corporate lives. One co-facilitator could ask the discussion questions to help the group as a whole glean truth from the passage, then the other co-facilitator could share an exhortation which summarizes what God has been saying through and to the group, with a focus on calling the group to put the discovered truths into practice together. Co-facilitators could alternate these roles from study to study or stick to their strengths each study.

APPLY: Pray & Act.
A summary is the perfect bridge from the interpret to the apply step. It gives a brief and clear look at the truths that we need to align our lives with. Understanding is not enough. In fact, brain research now shows that acting on knowledge is essential to knowing it fully. And although you'll likely only discuss 1-3 application questions, this step is so important to truly following Jesus who said in Luke 11:28: "Blessed rather are those who hear the word of God and obey it." The Bible says that hearing without obeying is dangerous, nurtures pride, and invites God's judgment! "From everyone who has been given much, much will be demanded" (Luke 12:48). So, leave enough time to discuss and pray over your applications. Ideally, some applications will relate to the justice work you are doing together, inspiring and directing group action. With the Bible being written to communities of God's people, help your group to apply it to both individual and group life. Action and prayer go hand-in-hand. God strengthens us and directs our action as we pray. Be specific in your applications – in both prayer and action.

You've Got This!
Our prayer is that helping your Beloved Community grow in this inductive approach will let the Bible speak for itself so that you can faithfully observe, interpret and apply it to your individual and corporate lives. You are essential as a facilitator, but God's Word has the power to transform. Keep it central!

Asking Effective Questions

"Forming good questions about the text is a key to interpretation. The heart of good inductive Bible study should be the forming of good questions about the text, questions which will probe the depths of the text and uncover layers of meaning which may not appear on the surface." - *Enhancements to Inductive Bible Study*, by the InterVarsity Christian Fellowship/USA Bible Study Task Force, April 1999.

Good Questions Should...
1. be real questions - not with completely obvious answers.
2. help people discover and understand the central truths of the text.
3. be clear and concise; not so complex that they are difficult to understand.
4. be phrased in the language of the group and the text.
5. stimulate the group to think deeply about the text's meaning.
6. be true discussion questions (open-ended rather than yes/no questions) with multiple answers.
7. encourage the group to look back into the text (rather than only expressing their opinions).
8. not be merely speculative but be answerable in the text and/or the wider textual and cultural context.
9. help the group to link their own life experience to the text.

10. help the group make sense of connections (repetition, contrast, etc) they've found in the text.
11. help the group probe the perspectives, motives, and emotions of the author, recipients, and characters.
12. lead to valuable discussion, focusing on important themes, not incidental details.
13. include those which naturally come to mind upon reading the text (anticipating the group's questions).

Bonding Questions

1. Which verse of Scripture best expresses your hopes for our Beloved community? (show foundations Scriptures as a reference)
2. What was your sweetest experience of multiracial fellowship?
3. Think of a close community you've been a part of; what made it so special?
4. As a child, when did you first notice people of another race or language? What helped you interpret those differences?
5. What experience of yours reveals the depth of our racial brokenness?
6. What is something unusual about a sibling or cousin of yours?
7. What is your "life verse" and why?
8. Which Scripture gave you guidance or comfort at an important juncture in your life?
9. Tell us about a time when you sensed clear direction from the Lord or a time when you had to make a big decision without being confident of which course was best.
10. Tell us about a time when something happened which clearly revealed God's intervention.
11. What is something you created that was a satisfying use of your talents?
12. What family member are you closest to and why?
13. What traits do you most value in a friend?
14. In what way are you most often misunderstood?

15. What character traits would you like to grow in?
16. If you had 10 more hours added to your week, what would you do with them?
17. What trait do you most wish will rub off on you from others?
18. Which single habit has helped you grow the most?
19. What are some of your long-term goals in life?
20. Aside from Jesus Christ, who do you most want to emulate?
21. What is your earliest memory?
22. What is a memory you wish you could forget?
23. What painful season in your life are you now grateful for?
24. What fictional book or film character do you most admire?
25. If you were to spend a year in the wilderness, what three non-essential items would you bring (other than food, clothes, shelter and survival gear) and why?
26. If you could have one super power, what would it be and why?
27. Aside from Jesus Christ, what biblical character would you like to be more like?
28. What biblical command do you find hardest to follow?
29. What biblical promise do you most long for?
30. What work would you like to do in the new heavens and the new earth?
31. What aspect of the fruit of the Spirit do you most need to grow in?
32. What has been your biggest challenge in life?
33. What has helped you move from being self-centered to being others-centered?
34. What has helped you grow in humility?
35. Tell us about your mentor.
36. Tell us about a relationship which has been both challenging and rewarding.
37. Would you rather have a little more…

a. Patience or energy?
   b. Smarts or resilience?
   c. Money or time?
   d. Work or free time?
   e. Wealth or longevity?
   f. Family or friends?
   g. Talent or influence?
38. What lives are you best suited to impact?
39. Who do you miss the most?
40. Tell us about an enjoyable and fruitful collaboration.
41. When do you feel closest to God?
42. What is your relationship to music like?
43. What is a fear you hope to conquer?
44. What are you obsessed with or addicted to?
45. What are you afraid to tell us?
46. What about yourself do you dislike the most?
47. What was the best day, week and year of your life?
48. What are your favorite three books?
49. What is your favorite genre of books?
50. What book would you like to write?
51. What is a key insight which has profoundly shaped your life?
52. In what ways are you different than you were 10 years ago?
53. What advice do you wish you could give the 20-year-old you?
54. What lasting contribution do you want your life to make?
55. What injustices is do you feel led to expose and oppose?
56. Tell us about a time you experienced solidarity with suffering people. How did it change you?
57. What is your most impossible dream?
58. What is your biggest regret and have you come to peace with it?
59. What is your biggest disappointment and how has it shaped you?

60. What is the most unexpected turn your life has taken and how do you feel about it?
61. What word or deed of your parents made the biggest impact on your life?
62. What have you learned from the children in your life?
63. Tell us about a broken relationship that has been healed or one that you wish was healed.
64. When do you feel most alive?
65. If you had an extra $100,000, what would you do with it?
66. Tell us about a scar on your body.
67. If you had to get a tattoo today, what would it be?
68. What are your greatest strengths and weaknesses?
69. What is your life purpose?
70. What is your vocational calling and to what degree are you on track to fulfilling it?
71. What was the biggest turning point that preceded your beginning to follow Jesus?
72. What are the major milestones in your spiritual journey?
73. How did you come to have a heart for serving the poor?
74. What was your first answer to prayer?
75. Reflect on people you have admired or even envied; what does it reveal about your deepest aspirations?
76. What is something you have struggled with in the last few months?
77. Do you act very differently when among different types of people? Why or why not?
78. Tell us about a turning point in your relationship or mindset toward the opposite sex?

Evaluating My Bible Study Facilitation

METHOD
<u>Was I true to the inductive bible study method?</u>

a. Did I lead the group effectively through each step: Observe, Interpret, Apply?

b. Did I show how textual and cultural contexts illuminate the text?

c. Did I give them time and encouragement to look closely at the passage?

d. Did I ask for the group's questions and observations and did I take them seriously?

e. Did I give them time and encouragement to look closely at the passage?

f. Did I help the group stay focused on *this* particular passage?

g. Did I help the group discover the central message of the text?

h. Did I summarize what the group discovered to be the central message?

i. Did I help the group to choose a clear and specific response that was relevant to the vision and mission of Beloved Communities?

j. Was my prep time in the passage adequate?

QUESTIONS
<u>Were my questions effective?</u>

a. Were they true discussion questions (not yes/no or completely obvious)?

b. Were my questions clear and concise?

c. Did I pose enough questions to keep the group wrestling with the main themes?

d. Did my questions stimulate the group to think deeply about the text's meaning?

CARE
<u>Did I care for the group members by creating an atmosphere of openness and trust?</u>

    a. Did I affirm people's responses?

    b. Did I use questions that have only one answer? ("What I was really looking for was…")

    c. Did people feel free to share their thoughts without fear of giving the wrong answer?

    d. Did I let anyone's response change the course of discussion?

    e. Did I build on what others said during the discussion or was it all about what I'd seen in the passage?

    f. Did I invite shy group members into the conversation?

LEADERSHIP
<u>Did I exert the right amount of leadership?</u>

    a. Did I let the group follow too many "rabbit trails?"

b. Did I speak after each person's response or did I let the discussion flow without me when the group was "on track?"

c. Did I feel compelled to answer all of my own questions?

d. Did I dominate the discussion? What percentage of the time was I talking?

e. Did I demonstrate a healthy balance of freedom and direction?

f. How was the pace? Did I sense when it was important to linger on a point and when it was time to move on?

HUMILITY
Did I have a posture of humility?

a. Did I presume to thoroughly understand the passage, or did I come as a learner myself?

b. Did I expect and seek to learn from the group members?

c. Did I let the Scripture be the authority, freeing me to say "I don't know…what do you guys think?"

Evaluating My Bible Study Facilitation

    d. Did I set a tone of openness by being vulnerable with how the passage exposed my own sins and shortcomings?

    _____

    e. Did I realize that my racial and gender blindspots may skew my understanding of the passage? Did I listen for the Spirit to expose and correct blindspots through the perspective of others?

    _____

INCLUSION
<u>Was I aware of racial and gender dynamics within the group and seek to be a bridge builder?</u>

    a. Did I promote Beloved's Value of "prioritizing the voices of people of color and women" by inviting any missing voices into the discussion?

    _____

    b. Did I make time for a final exhortation that summarized the central theme of this discussion (to balance traditionally Black and White approaches to bible study)?

    _____

    c. Did I affirm the words of attendees whose gender and ethnicity are different from my own?

    _____

    d. Did I handle any racially sensitive topics with grace and truth?

    _____

The battlefield requires a directive leadership style, but our leaders see themselves as facilitators who set the stage for the members to invest in each other.

FACILITATOR	VS.	COMMANDER
Make group central		Make self central
Build community		Build authority
Help members discover what to do		Tell members what to do
Bring out the wisdom of the group		Showcase own expertise
Help members find their voices		Dominate with own voice
Maintain guidelines		Control discussion
Add value		Sell services
Serve the group		Direct the group

Connecting with Beloved Communities Inc

Are You Ready to Build Unity Between Believers Across the Color Line?

If so, choose your level of connection with us:

    A. LAUNCH A BELOVED COMMUNITY.

Start a group where you live and connect online with other facilitators for mutual learning and support. Learn more at www.Beloved-Communities.org then connect with us at info@beloved-communities.org. We hope you'll consider becoming a leader in this movement of Christ-centered, multiracial, cross-congregational small groups. See our vision, mission, values and key actions below.

    B. USE OUR TOOLS.

Adapt some of our tools as they fit with what you're doing. You can always go all-in with Beloved Communities later! Explore our library at www.Beloved-Communities.org which contains dozens of free downloadable tools in these categories:

1. Racial Healing
2. Launching Your Own Beloved Community
3. Facilitating Discussions
4. Applying to Lead
5. About Beloved Communities Inc

Please share your stories on the Beloved Communities Facebook page of how this bible study guide has been a blessing. We'd also love to see photos of your group studying, praying, fellowshipping and working together for biblical justice. May God "establish the work of [y]our hands" (Psalm 90:17)!

Values:

Pursuit of Truth – facing and healing our hard history.

Multiracial Friendship – enjoying the unity we share in Christ.

Authentic Witness – loving each other draws people to King Jesus.

Shared Leadership – prioritizing the voices of people of color and women.

Biblical Justice – praying and acting for positive change.

Beloved Communities is a movement of Christ-centered, multiracial, cross-congregational small groups which embrace...

Vision: a racially healing Body of Christ.

Mission: Enjoy multiracial friendships focused on biblical justice.

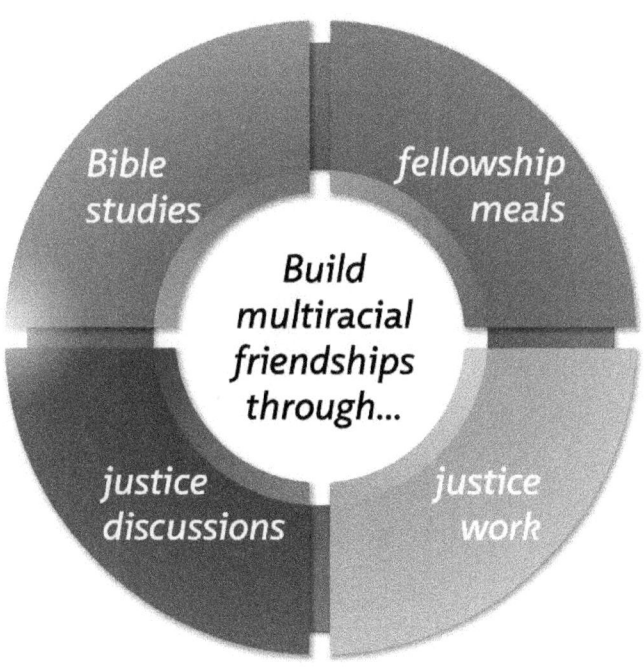

Works Cited

Adeyemo, T. *Africa Bible Commentary*. Nairobi, Zondervan, 2006.

Beloved Communities. *Beloved Communities.org*, Beloved Communities Inc, www.Beloved-Communities.org.

Carson, D. A. *New Bible Commentary*. Leicester, InterVarsity Press, 1953.

Kirk, L.T. *Justice and Mercy*. Sermon, Christ Community Church, Daytona Beach, FL, November 26, 2006.

Labberton, M. *The Dangerous Act of Worship*. Downers Grove, InterVarsity Press, 2007.

Lewis, Jacqui. "Freedom, Liberty, and Justice for All." *Sojourners Magazine*, January 2021, p. 24.

USA Bible Study Task Force. *Enhancements to Inductive Bible Study*. April ed., Intervarsity Christian Fellowship, 1999.

Walton, J., Matthews, V., Chavalas, M. *The IVP Bible Background Commentary: Old Testament*. Downers Grove, InterVarsity Press, 2000.

Young, E. *The Book of Isaiah: Volume 3*. Grand Rapids, Eerdmans, 1997

www.ingramcontent.com/pod-product-compliance
Lightning Source LLC
Chambersburg PA
CBHW071739040426
42446CB00012B/2398